My Teen Friend

My Teen Friend

The Courage to be a Teen

By Sunee Grace

Published by Wiser Day on Earth

Byron Bay, New South Wales

Australia

www.wiserdayonearth.com

ISBN: 978-1-7643315-0-0

Many thanks for the graphic design and formatting by Liliana Gonzalez who can be contacted at bookmakerfactory.comte

All of the photos in this book were taken in Australia.

Many thanks to my friends and the Photographers who helped to give life to my book, including...

The front cover featuring Samara, Sam, Oskar, Arky & myself Sunee, and the back cover, both photographed by Nelly le Comte.

Branches 20 and 21 photographed by Jade Goldberg.

Branch 5 photographed by Crystal Wilkes.

And Branches 6, 9, 16, 29, 32, 34, 37 and 45 photographed by Aaron Beth'el,

All other photos taken by Sunee Grace.

Finally, please check out my album on Spotify, Sunee Grace, "Chosen Moments."

Author Bio

Hi, My name is Sunee and I'm a teenager, living near the coast of northern New South Wales, Australia.

I am currently homeschooled and I love it.

I am a writer, a singer, and I play the keyboard and compose songs. I also love photography, drama, dancing, cooking, and going to the gym. I guess something a little more unusual about me is that I can communicate with animals.

When I was three, I wrote stories and listened to my Dad telling me stories as well. I have always been into writing, whether it's essays for school, writing contemplations in my own time, or composing songs, poems and haikus.

Writing has given me a sense of freedom and being able to forget about my worries. I lose myself in a beautiful bubble, where it's just me and my book or computer, and there I write from my heart, for a period of creative time.

I remember the first day I said, "I want to write a book." It feels like a long time ago, yet I have learnt so much about myself through this process, and now I know that I do have the capacity and strength to write a book.

As you can probably tell, I'm very passionate about writing, and English remains one of my favourite subjects.

I'm excited for you to experience my book and get to know me a little more on your reading journey. Remember, it's not just my book, it's yours too!

Dedication & thanks

I dedicate this book to my amazing parents Tanya and Aaron, my Nana Danielle and Papa Steve, and all of my wonderful family and friends in Australia, the US and UK.

I feel so lucky and inspired by all of these people who have made a deep mark of love in my life, and I am forever grateful to them.

I also want to thank Samara, Sam, Oskar, and Arky for a great afternoon spent at the beach taking photos for the book cover.

Contents

Introduction 1

Branch 1. Being in the Present Moment 3
Branch 2. Beauty 7
Branch 3. Nature 11
Branch 4. Love 15
Branch 5. Kindness 19
Branch 6. Embracing Life 23
Branch 7. We and the Earth 27
Branch 8. Friendship 31
Branch 9. Being an Individual 35
Branch 10. Visions 39
Branch 11. Patience 43
Branch 12. Vitality for Life 47
Branch 13. Confidence 51
Branch 14. Why We Are Here 55
Branch 15. Abundance 59
Branch 16. Protection 63
Branch 17. Reality 67

Branch 18. Point of View 71
Branch 19. Wisdom 75
Branch 20. Acceptance 79
Branch 21. Freedom 83
Branch 22. Peace 87
Branch 23. Happiness 91
Branch 24. Wellbeing 95
Branch 25. Perfect 99
Branch 26. Negative Thoughts 103
Branch 27. Judgment 107
Branch 28. Intuition 111
Branch 29. Being Upset 115
Branch 30. Compassion 119
Branch 31. Life is Short 122
Branch 32. Finding our True Selves 127
Branch 33. Self-Esteem 131
Branch 34. Bullying 135
Branch 35. Controlling 139
Branch 36. Food 143
Branch 37. Decision Making 147
Branch 38. Taking Risks 151
Branch 39. Spirituality 155
Branch 40. Beliefs 159
Branch 41. Community 163
Branch 42. Wanting More 167
Branch 43. Positivity 171
Branch 44. What's Real or Fake 175
Branch 45. Anger 178

Branch 46. Harmony 183
Branch 47. Quiet Moments 187
Branch 48. Laughter 191
Branch 49. Self-Reflection 195
Branch 50. Truth 199
Branch 51. Maturity 202
Branch 52. Wonders of Life 207

Introduction

I created 'My Teen Friend' to inspire you, so that you don't feel alone on your life journey.

During this stage of life, we experience similar struggles, and I hope that you will turn to this book for a little guidance and love.

In each branch of 'My Teen Friend,' I have added a photo as well as a poem.

There are 52 branches in the book, one for each week of the year, which means that if you wanted to get more from the book, then you could focus on one branch a week. However, its entirely up to you, how you read this book.

Regardless of what you gain from it, I want you to remember that I wrote this book to heal and inspire, and I hope that is exactly what it does.

Branch 1

Being in the Present Moment

I first became aware of being in the present moment with my Dad many years ago. We had slowly created a painting, without thinking, and just let the paintbrush take over.

Afterwards, we went for a walk, and with each step, we slowly walked with awareness. I noticed so much life around us, every little touch of the plants against my legs, the sun shining on me and the birds singing in the background. It was a real eye-opener. It opened my world and expanded it in more ways than I could imagine or explain.

So the first thing about being in the present moment is to accept and feel content about who we are, while focusing on what is happening now, not later, and not before now.

Then we can fully connect on a deeper level and live peacefully in our mind and body, at ease with ourselves and our surroundings.

Being in the present moment is timeless, and some people find it difficult. But for me, if I overthink life too much, then I won't fully experience it, so I always try to return my thoughts to now.

If you ever feel out of balance, being in the present moment is a good way to return to yourself.

Poem on
Being in the Present Moment

Being present makes us happy and aware
when we connect with ourselves
someone, or something else.
Being present gives us a time and a place
to let our awareness grow to a deeper level.
Like a river pouring out to sea
our presence in the moment
bubbles into infinite depths
both here and beyond
at the same time.

Branch 2

Beauty

Beauty is why I believe all of us are here. As souls, we noticed a beautiful Earth and dived into it.

We are here to experience the beauty of others, and others are here to experience our beauty.

Beauty is simple, but we take it for granted. There is beauty in all of us, whether it comes from the outside or the inside.

I also think about the many people in the world living, loving, crying, sleeping, hurting and dying, though most of the time we aren't aware of other's pain and hurt.

We are all stuck in our little bubbles that we rarely pop .

Yet beauty also passes, though it wants to flower between us all, since much of the time we aren't aware of living in a world of beauty. We just need to breathe the air of beautiful fresh perspectives.

Poem on
Beauty

Rarely do we see true beauty

within ourselves

or even the world.

Something so fragile

can be so pretty and dainty,

but we ignore or forget it.

Yet we can see and feel beauty

when the eyes of our soul

and the presence of our heart

are open.

Branch 3

Nature

Without nature, there wouldn't be peaceful green forests, snow-topped mountains, blue skies and oceans, beautiful animals and people.

Nature is the greatest cure of all.

When I get sick, I feel more drawn to nature, it's almost like the pull of gravity, with the trees saying, "Come to us Sunee, we will make you better." And so I find a tree and sit with my back against it.

When we wander into nature, we feel life, love and peace returning us to the present moment.

When we are in nature, we often just 'see' but if we look deeply, we open our heart, as well as our eyes. Then we realise that nature has awakened our soul, to connect with our own nature through its' beauty.

Poem on Nature

Petals upwardly loving
touching velvet blue skies
downwardly shining.
Pollen arrives
sweetly on time
blossoming lands
with colours divine.
Oceans, lakes, rivers
rising and falling
flowing light crossing
waving between all.
Nature's eyes everywhere
touching deeply in mind.
Soft pastel mountains
piercing heaven above
opening joy further
reaching hearts of love.

Branch 4

Love

Love is powerful...

It involves being secure yet vulnerable, and includes both giving, as well as receiving.

To love is to connect on a deeper level and feel joy.

The more love we give through our thoughts, words, feelings and body language, the more we will create a happier, safer and kinder world.

After every encounter with love, we are left with a little electric feeling that just feels so right, and that all is well in our world.

Love embraces our precious moments and makes them last forever, so we can connect to ourselves, others and nature.

However, if we do love someone, it doesn't mean that everything is great.

Love can make it harder once we know someone is in love with us. It might make us feel we have to commit more than we may want, as we feel pressure to say, "I love you," even if we don't fully feel that way.

So love is about trusting ourselves and to know deep down what we truly feel.

What do you think love is?

Poem on
Love

Walking through nature we know what love is
for we feel love's smile inside.
Love travels in circles
flowing out and returning.
Love for our world
caring for the land
and magically
they return love to us.
Circulating oceans and realms
love spreads beyond all knowing.
Love, compassion and kindness
join us to life, humanity
and to the stars.

Branch 5

Kindness

Kindness can instantly change a person's perspective about life. It's about spreading love to others, and of course to ourselves too.

Sometimes we may feel that we are not being kind enough, so as soon as we feel that way, we can change the way we act.

I believe that acts of kindness go a long way. We can brighten another's face with our smile and create a loving feeling with those we meet.

Even small acts of kindness can go a long way, and in turn, help others feel more connected and inspired to be kind to someone else.

The other day after waiting twenty minutes for my takeout dumplings I walked past a homeless man sitting on the sidewalk with his dog, and gave the dumplings to him. He gave me the biggest smile and thank you, and I no longer felt hungry. His smile made my day.

The kinder we are, the more the world will change into a happier and more loving place. When I notice that someone needs a little kindness, I smile, talk or sometimes even give them something.

The best feeling after the action of being kind is the impact it has on us. It makes our day and it can make someone else's.

What happens when you experience kindness?

Poem on
Kindness

Kindness spreads love
while freeing our worries
so we can give more to others.
Kindness is most powerful
when we deeply care
for each other.
Kindness brings us together
and makes us feel happy
as human beings.
Our kind love
flies into the heart of nature
and returns an ancient kindness
that we can treasure.

Branch 6
Embracing Life

When we embrace life, not only is a space created in our heads and hands for openness, but a state of awareness is also created in our hearts.

We could call it, "Awareness of life's beauty."

When we acknowledge our surroundings, we start to see everything in a different, more enhanced light. We have insights and see the colours of love in different ways, and most of all, we truly live in the present moment.

It's a special gift to become aware of life, with its ever-flowing creativity.

If we embrace life, it allows us to open our minds and let things go.

We become part of something bigger.

We feel love and acceptance, and gain an awareness of being embraced by nature.

How do you embrace life?

Poem on
Embracing Life

Life is full of new experiences
when we choose worthy adventures.
Exploring our world
in an open and meaningful way
is to embrace more life
and more of our true selves.

Branch 7

We and the Earth

This is our Earth, and we are the people of Earth.

We arrived aeons ago.

We might think we have some knowledge about the world, but the reality is, it depends upon what we believe.

We can all interpret life very differently from each other.

The Australian Aboriginals teach us that we can remember our ancestors by continuing their traditions, such as dancing, feeling the earth, and passing on stories to the younger generation. They believe that this knowledge can be passed on…

and on and on.

It's important to be grateful for everything we have, regardless of what it is.

We can always find something to be grateful for, though sometimes we may need to open our minds towards larger horizons.

Poem on
We and the Earth

Can we feel the Earth

and its opening forces

filling us with awareness

truth and love?

So we can become

what we have always been

beyond the surface

and from amongst the stars.

Branch 8
Friendship

Everyone struggles with friendships at some point in life. And yet, the world is full of amazing people that we can learn and grow from.

Our time on Earth is precious, so let's use it wisely.

When I went to school, I struggled to make friends. I didn't fit in, I was too different. Everyone was interested in things that I didn't find interesting. So I stuck to myself and would end up in the junior classrooms, because the teachers could see I was struggling.

Now, I want to inspire you to continue on your life journey, regardless of what might happen.

I may have struggled at school, but now I am stronger and know my worth, because I've learnt so much from these experiences.

Being a good friend means everything to me. I love caring for my friends and I'm proud to have their backs.

Being there for someone can mean a lot, so if you can, do it.

If we come across someone who is very much our person as a friend, don't let go of them and always make an effort.

If we are caring and loving, others will pick up on it, and they are more likely to make an effort too.

We don't have to literally say that we are a loving and kind person, instead, we can simply show them through our actions. Then, people will instantly know we are interested in getting to know them.

I hope you have, or will find great friends.

Poem on
Friendship

Even in a winter garden
friends can warm cold hearts
and open distant minds.
Blossoms blossom best in a gentle garden
spreading out to hold each other's hands.
Opening new horizons
through flowering smiles with friendly eyes.

Branch 9
Being an Individual

Growing up, we look to people who seem to be together, whether it's older siblings, parents, other family members, friends or teachers.

As we grow older, we start to notice changes in the way we talk, act and respond.

Slowly, we realise who we are becoming, how we respond or answer to others, and what we want, as we become more of the person we want to be.

It's fascinating how the mind works and the decisions we all make.

All I know is that what I want to be is what I'm doing now, and I couldn't be more grateful to my parents for giving me the most amazing opportunities.

But don't worry if you're confused about who you are, because you will find yourself one day, and then, you'll know the unique reason why you are here.

Being unique is important, it lets everyone know that you, we, all of us, have our own voice, and we aren't just going to agree with everything that other people say.

All ages deserve a voice, and to speak up, and be who they are meant to be.

I'm happiest when I'm being myself. But if I'm not alone enough, I can sometimes lose myself. Yet, pretty much straight away I can tell that I'm not being uniquely me.

What makes you uniquely you?

Poem on
Being an Individual

Individuality grows through inner strength
self-love and feeling.
The love of true connections
occurs best
while choosing our path
through the unique eyes
of our true self.

Branch 10

Visions

Sometimes, I see my whole life in front of my inner eyes, and I find myself looking into my past, present and future, flowing through time. When I have this kind of vision, I know what I want.

At times, our dreams can feel just as life-like.

It's as if our visions and dreams are here to show us something special that is important for us to know.

To think about what we want to do in the outside world can seem hard at times, but if we have an inner goal that we would like to create, even if we may not know all the steps needed to make it a reality, we can instead use our imaginary vision around what we want, and it might come in the most unexpected way.

Our visions call to us, so that we may see into other worlds, where we feel a bubbling creativity that awakens our awareness to blossom with life here on Earth.

Poem on

Visions

Let's open the window of our minds
to the wonders above the skies.
For visions call us beyond our daily life
to explore and meet the unknown.

Branch 11

Patience

If we are patient, we can enjoy the innocent and natural things in life, as well as notice the Earth from new perspectives.

Patience makes us a more balanced human being, and a more aware one too.

We will certainly feel a change in ourselves if we slow down from our busy lives and just be in the present moment.

Patience comes with kindness, love, wisdom, and most of all, being able to stop and feel the bare earth beneath us, as well as everything around us.

Others will want to spend time with you, if you live patiently, in a more aware place.

Poem on
Patience

Patience is waiting inside of us.
The deeper we can see within
the higher we can bloom
to patiently embrace life.

Branch 12

Vitality for Life

When we feel down, we often believe there is no space for our heart to take in more. Maybe we are sick of the same dramas or routine, or we have no positive thoughts coming into our minds.

We might look at things negatively and think, "What's the point?" Sometimes I feel like that when I haven't seen anyone for a while, or I haven't done much during the week and I feel down and grumpy.

But that's where we can go wrong.

We need to get off our phones, look outside and realise there is an abundance of life in the world.

There is so much to see and explore, including within ourselves.

Deep down, we all have a bubbling well of vitality that wants to rise to the surface in our life.

Vitality is a special word. The first part of the word is Vital, which means essential for life, therefore vitality is life, with added enthusiasm.

Through vitality, we can truly live and explore our dreams on Earth, and I hope you regularly experience the flowering vitality of life.

Poem on
Vitality for Life

Vitality is everywhere.

We see it as the sun

breaks through the clouds at dawn.

When rain falls upon parched land.

When ocean waves

tumble into surf upon the shore.

When the wind whistles

through forests and across mountains.

When a seedling

breaks through the soil

or when a child is born…

Branch 13

Confidence

To be more confident, we have to know who we are. If we don't, we won't be able to put our best selves forward.

Yet even then, we may still be fearful.

It's important to try and picture yourself doing something out of your comfort zone, yet doing it with a big smile and doing it successfully.

We should also be respectful to those around us. This can create respect within ourselves and also inspire others to do the same. In this way, we get to believe that we are good enough, as we continue to build our character inside.

Following this, we can become more sure of who we are, and what we want to do and create in the world. We can do anything if we set our minds to it, but we may need to remember not to get overly confident and become big-headed.

We can open up to others about our experiences and practice being confident. This can inspire people and make them feel that they are not alone, because everybody goes through awkwardness and lack of confidence at some point in their lives.

A good place to start is to question, where and when do you feel most confident, even just a little, and take it from there.

Poem on
Confidence

Courage and confidence arise from the same stream.

They arise from the highest mountains

and flow into our lives with energy, power and direction.

When we are confident, we are like mountaineers

we stand tall

we tread mindfully

and we focus on our breath.

Branch 14

Why We Are Here

I believe we are all here for a reason.

We all came at different times and landed at different places. Yet, we came at the right time for ourselves and those around us.

Sometimes we may not feel like we belong here and wonder why we came. But the thing is, we may not know the reason right now, and that's okay. But I think we're supposed to discover this on our journey, as we explore who we are.

When I think about the world, I feel it's such a special place to be, and I'm glad I was given the gift to come here and meet my people.

Poem on
Why We Are Here

We came to Earth

to find who we are.

To respect all life

the land and its people.

So we may discover

our natural reality

and what's real…

Branch 15
Abundance

Living with abundance is simply embracing life through having fun and letting joy into our daily lives. It's also about making peace within ourselves, and towards others, as well as the world.

When I hear or say 'Abundance', I feel a kind of electric happiness, and it reminds me of a ball of vibrant colours!

So abundance is really about living life with positivity, adventure, peace, love and most of all, having fun-loving moments so that we create precious memories.

We can begin embracing the abundance of life with anything at all, whether a sunrise or sunset, a raindrop, a smile, an apple, or a friend.

Poem on

Abundance

Life abundantly come to us
love, peace and fun come too.
And memories allow us to feel
precious times once again
as we forever hold those thought seeds
in deep and bountiful lands.

Branch 16

Protection

It's very important to protect and to be protected by our loved ones. To tune into others and feel that deep down they are good people. We also need people we can rely on and feel safe with.

But there are a few not-so-good, or maybe ignorant people in the world. When I say this, I don't want to define them as bad. It's just that sometimes if we have seen or heard something bad about others, we may emphasise that. But they may be going through something that no one would ever know or realise.

So just as it's important not to judge a book by its cover, it's also important not to pre-judge a seemingly not-so-good person or someone with a bad history.

I mean, we could make a new friend, yet have no idea who they were before.

Things happen and everyone has issues. But if we can move on, we can all live our lives more freely and peacefully.

Poem on

Protection

Light is always our friend.
The sun or a candle protects us
from dark and scary thoughts.
Awakening our illusions
and allowing us
to peacefully return to happiness.

Branch 17

Reality

Reality is life. It's the day to day life we live, even though everyone looks at the world a little differently from everyone else.

The reality we think we live in, is what we know.

However, if you look deeply at how you live your life, you may realise you are slowly building your own tower of experience that is reaching ever higher, so you can build a better view and understand more about life.

Yet, reality can also wake us from being in different places in our mind or body.

It can then make us feel determined to take action, especially if we suddenly realise we are stuck, limited, or that what we've been thinking may not have been a true reality.

Poem on
Reality

Our thoughts can sometimes be all-consuming
yet suddenly a moment of stillness occurs
and a sprout of awareness
breaks through the surface
reminding us to return to reality
from where our love
can blossom and spread outwards.

Branch 18

Point of View

To have a truly known point of view, we have to know who we are and what we want in the world, and that can sometimes take a long time.

When I think of different points of view, we may not agree with everything that another says, and that's okay.

Sometimes, we may need to keep our own opinions to ourselves and perhaps just share them with those we respect.

I feel that people do judge me for things in life, like being a vegetarian. I get asked a lot of questions like, "Would you eat a tiny piece of meat for a million dollars?" I dislike these questions. I always say I would never eat meat, yet unfortunately, some people just don't understand and judge me for it. But that is their opinion.

I try not to fall into a similar judgement about them, by thinking how could they eat the life of an animal. After all, animals are like us, they want to live, and they deserve to live their life.

When I think about, "Point of View" I feel a little nervous to be honest, because I may be exposing myself to the judgments of others. But I also feel strong at the same time, knowing that I know what I believe, and understand the qualities I want to bring to this world.

My friends and family know who I am, what my values are, and what they mean to me as a human being.

So, let's not be scared to be ourselves, and instead, learn to adapt, stand tall and be proud of who we are, and who we are becoming.

Poem on
Point of View

We are here looking outwards.
through different eyes and windows
seeing different views of reality.
Oceans turn their tides
trusting themselves
knowing they are right.
Clouds sail
to anchor above
their chosen valley.
Trees stand tall
naturally confident
in their point of view.
And so can we...

Branch 19

Wisdom

Wisdom is special to me, because a lot of wisdom and love lives in my house, every day I'm with my family.

When we say the word "Wisdom" you probably think of wise sayings and wise actions, or wise people who lived in the past, and all of them living with a clear headspace.

But I think the most important thing about wisdom, is that it has the power to change our perspective on how we view the world, and how we can make wiser decisions in our everyday lives.

Everyone has a sense of wisdom in different ways to others, but it doesn't mean they are better, it just means they have different ways of looking at how life is.

I love to be in nature, because time slows down for me, and I start to see the world a little differently, especially when I open my eyes to the smallest living things.

Then I remember, once again to have more appreciation for the wisdom of our beautiful Earth.

I love to speak from the heart of my experiences, by writing poems and songs to express my love for the world.

I hope that you too also see and appreciate wisdom, even in the tiniest things, as I believe our world would be very different and healthier in every way if we lived with greater wisdom.

Poem on Wisdom

Opening our eyes to the stream of life
generously revealing wisdom.
Noticing innocent beauty and love
beyond everyday thoughts.
Living in electric moments
shivering down spines.
Connecting to tiny beings
we hadn't noticed before
in our shared world.

Branch 20

Acceptance

By accepting the truth of things or people, we are automatically going to live better lives, and develop empathy towards others and their story.

But acceptance isn't just about accepting others, it's also about accepting ourselves for who and what we are.

To be accepting of true choices shows that we are mature, kind and forgiving, which allows us to realise the truth about deeper situations.

When we create or see a positive change, this positivity becomes magnetic and can be instantly shared. Yet, when we feel disappointed in ourselves, it's also important to let go and forgive ourselves.

By accepting who we are, we can move on and live life, as well as notice the beauty that lies beyond our previously limited views.

Poem on
Acceptance

When a flower comes into our space
we can let it peacefully pass
with our accepting grace.
For acceptance
can travel between dimensions
even through times of pain and loss.
But mostly we can accept changes
in ourselves
that may reach
even beyond life.

Branch 21

Freedom

Among all the topics I have discussed, 'Freedom' is one of my favourites.

The word 'FREEDOM' is freeing! I instantly feel at ease, yet also excited, when I hear that word.

We have the freedom to be curious, to explore our world, and to make new friends and relationships. To do adventurous, fun things, and to feel free to do almost anything.

When we reach a certain age, we begin to see how much freedom we have. It can be terrifying, but also really exciting at the same time.

I'm coming to an age where people are starting to talk about my future and ask me questions. I am super excited to feel this bigger freedom, to live life to the fullest, and not have to ask my parents to take me, or drive me to places.

How about you? What does freedom mean to you in your world?

Freedom can bring happiness, creativity, a larger stage to play on, and most of all, change!

Poem on
Freedom

Let's stop drifting

turn the engine of life to cruising

or even up high

to see ourselves driving to a great future.

We know we never wanted to leave home

and yet we will

because new horizons call us.

Branch 22

Peace

Peace is what lies deep inside us.

At times we may not feel at peace because of our busy lives and routines. But when we take a break and step back, we will see the peace we have missed.

Peace is a beautiful, relaxing feeling, that enables us to enjoy the goodness and beauty of our world.

Without peace, we wouldn't have any realisation about our busy life, because we are so attached to routine and don't realise we are often living in a bubble filled with stress, sadness, fear or anger.

When we break out of our busy bubble, we notice a change in our manner, and that is when we become aware of our previous behaviour, and can then live more in the present.

Sometimes when I'm in my room I'll play ambient music, lie down on my bed and close my eyes, and very soon peace naturally appears.

Poem on
Peace

Peace lies within

above, below and beyond us all.

It is present before and after all storms.

And we remember

and are refreshed by peace

while it renews us

to live a peaceful life once again.

Branch 23

Happiness

I love the saying, "Fake it till you make it." I think it completely makes sense, and I know that it works with happiness too.

If you put a smile on your face, you will immediately feel happier, even if you are faking it to begin with, because if you continue to smile, I'm telling you, you will actually feel happier.

Happiness can come from something small to something bigger than the stars.

When people talk about happiness, many think that to live a perfect life, they need to be happy with their lives all of the time. But who is happy with their life all of the time?

True happiness means just being happy for no reason in the present moment, and being at peace in our own space and surroundings, without having over the top expectations.

Therefore, you can create your happiness, you don't have to wait for someone else, or to get something you think will make you happy.

Everyone creates their happiness in different ways which is beautiful. Every look, smile, and laugh can give you the strength and happiness to begin or continue your journey.

When I envision my happy place, I often think of the ocean. The golden-coloured beaches, turquoise sea, and fish peacefully gliding past. This feels like the comforting, refreshing home of my happiness. How about you?

Poem on
Happiness

When we are happy
happiness glows throughout our body
because deep down inside
that is what we are.
Then our inner beauty shines further
through happy smiles
creating a language
we all naturally know.

Branch 24

Wellbeing

Wellbeing is about keeping our mind, body and spirit vibrant and filled with life.

It's best if we can keep our mind healthy and fresh for life's journey, because the body and spirit will follow suit.

With a good mental balance we can be aware of our choices and what we decide to do for our lives.

When I think of the word, "Wellbeing" I automatically feel inspired to be good to myself and keep my wellbeing high. Yet the thing about wellbeing is that to have a good mental and physical state, we have to be open to improving and looking after ourselves, and then we can look after others with our wellbeing.

Working on ourselves can also help us see the greater good in others and I also believe that gratitude extends our wellbeing.

As teens, you and I can be grateful for the support of our family and friends, as well as who we have become, and all that life has given to us for our wellbeing.

Poem on
Wellbeing

When we are born

we seem to know some things from before.

As we grow

we see life and its creations

stretching to infinity.

But caught in busy lives

sometimes we forget

and miss the wonder of mountains

valleys and oceans

sparkling before us.

Branch 25

Perfect

Perfect is a word that can make us feel scared and anxious. Yet, we only know so much, and we can only be so much.

Life isn't always a breeze, it can be difficult sometimes, and we have to learn and adapt to the fact that no one is perfect, and no one has the perfect life.

We may think rich or famous people have the most perfect life, but you know what? They don't. It may seem like it, but if you lived with them, got to know them, and saw what their life was actually like, you would notice how life can sometimes be hard for them too.

A few years ago my Dad said to me, "Practice makes perfect." And I said to him, "Perfect? Nothing is perfect, but instead, we could say, better." So from then on, our family have always said, "Practice makes better."

Poem on
Perfect

We see that everything is perfect
but also that nothing is perfect.
We see how a flower can suddenly look
less beautiful
and not so delicate
as we originally remembered it.
Its such a wonder
how perfect always unravels
into being perfectly imperfect.

Branch 26

Negative Thoughts

Negative thoughts can bring negativity into our daily lives. If we are often negative, it won't help our mental or physical state.

It can be beneficial if we learn from our mistakes or judgments, and see that we don't need to actually be so negative.

But if we mindlessly follow our negative thoughts, they are only going to make our lives more complicated and stressful.

To live in a more positive state, we can start to be grateful for the smaller things in life and to see that beauty is everywhere, even underneath the surface.

So let's try to be more positive and see life in more positive ways.

Poem on
Negative Thoughts

Negativity can build

with every thought

and every word if we allow it.

But we can also let in positivity

and open to beauty

and the wild.

Branch 27

Judgment

There is always going to be people judging others. Many of us judge from the moment we see or meet a person for the first time. It may be in a nice way, such as we like what they say, or the fact they dress well. Or it might be something negative, such as we don't like their voice, or we don't think they are being kind or generous.

Yet deep down, we don't know these people or their circumstances. Speaking truthfully, we probably need to learn to adapt and change some of our judgements, and not take negative judgments on board as being true, especially if we think we are also being judged by others.

Instead, we can stand tall, and respect and appreciate who we truly are, because those who judge us, do not truly know us.

When I used to be judged by people, I would get down on myself. But over the years, I have learnt not to let other people's judgments bother me too much.

I am proud of who I am and proud of my life's journey. After all, my life experiences have made me the person I am today, and part of that also led me to write this book!

Poem on
Judgment

Ignore the stares from others
and see beyond
to where we connect.
Above the Earth
we stand tall
amongst the stars
where everyone shines brightly.

Branch 28

Intuition

Intuition is having an inner realisation about someone, something or ourselves. We are simply tuning into a situation in life.

I love tuning in with others.

My Mum and I are very good at tuning into situations, and seeing what may happen, or knowing what someone might say or do.

When I tune in, I feel like I am getting to know someone more deeply and kindly.

Sometimes I have a dream about someone, and it feels so real, and the very next day I'll see them and it feels really strange.

A few days ago, I had a chatty dream with someone I don't usually talk with. and the next day, I saw them, but this time they were nicer than usual and we talked a lot more.

When we are intuitive, our minds and bodies are often tuning in to deeper perceptions, even while we are asleep, so that during the day we can follow our intuition.

Poem on

Intuition

Dreams arise

freeing our minds and bodies

revealing intuition

to show who we are

and who we can become.

Branch 29

Being Upset

Being upset is a state we all experience. But if we think about why we are upset, of course there are reasons, but are they good reasons? Or is it just about wanting to remain in control, being selfish, looking to blame someone, or avoiding a particular person?

When we have difficult arguments or issues with our family, loved ones and friends, it can sometimes be hard not to be upset, judge, or point the finger at them.

But I've learned that we are in charge of the way we make ourselves feel, so being upset is actually a choice. So the next time you are upset, try to not let it cloud how you actually feel. Eventually we may find that anything negative, including being upset, is not the full truth.

Time with family and friends is so valuable, and it's not forever. So instead of feeling upset and pointing the finger, try to use your creative mind to focus on something loving and happy, and look at the situation with a new perspective.

Poem on
Being Upset

Being upset sweeps away
the wonder of our lives.
When we open our eyes
and consider others
that's when we start to think
beyond the causes
of being upset.

Branch 30

Compassion

Compassion is having consideration and kindness for others, ourselves and all forms of life including animals, plants and insects.

When we live with compassion, we get to know ourselves more deeply, and naturally act with kindness. We can offer our love, kindness and smiles freely, because deep down we are made that way.

If we see someone who looks like they don't have much, or are homeless, we can try to be compassionate and lovingly offer them at least our smile, and maybe more.

A lot of people walk past homeless people without giving them a thought or take the time to say hello. But if we are not compassionate towards other people, then we are missing out on giving the love and kindness we have growing deep inside of us.

I have come across some people who are so compassionate that they give and give and give whatever they have. Whether it's offering cooked meals like my Mum, or helping others, like my Dad, every little act of compassion counts towards the greater good of humanity.

Surely we can give others our meaningful kindness and compassion.

Poem on
Compassion

Freeing compassion
from deep inside
so we can live it now
for this is our time to give.
By opening and offering
ourselves to others
we won't have to say
a sorry goodbye.

Branch 31

Life is Short

Life is short, but if we are grateful for the things that happen in our daily lives, then our time is not wasted. If we spend precious moments in the full presence of another's company, then our time is not wasted.

Yet when I think of life, I also think about death.

When I was younger, I used to over-think everything about death and be scared and cry about it. Every time I heard something horrible on the news, or of someone we knew who was hurt or very ill, I would always be deeply upset. But as I've grown older, I look at death in a lighter way. I don't instantly feel depressed, maybe still a little sad, but not really down.

Instead, I feel happy for the people and animals that have passed, and were in pain, because now their spirits are free, smiling between the stars.

My Granny Pauline passed away at the end of 2023. She was and still is a very, very special woman. She had so many flavours to her personality and it was always interesting and inspiring to have a conversation with her. Everyone who knew her was treated like her grandchild. She would give me and my friends pocket money, and they would call her Granny too.

The last day I had with my Granny felt very different to the usual. I couldn't quite describe it, but it just did. I was checking on her, and giving her a drink, because she had been living with us for the last couple of years, and mostly she had been confined to her bed. I remember feeling like it was going to be my last time giving her water, but I just ignored the thought. I kissed her on the cheek and said, "I'm going to go now Granny, love you" and then she smiled and looked up at me, although it was like she was

saying thank you and goodbye. She then said in a very soft and loving way, "I love you." Then I left, and I never saw her alive again.

After her passing, the thing I couldn't get out of my mind was the fact that just yesterday I was with her, and she was talking, and now she was gone, no more breathing, no more smiles, and no more seeing her divine blue eyes.

This was an experience I had never had, and in some ways, I am grateful that she passed in her sleep and was smiling until the end. Granny was, and still is the strongest and best Granny I could ever have.

Have you ever lost someone you loved? They may be gone, but the love remains.

Poem on
Life is Short

Living beyond words
living between worlds.
Letting earthly worries go.
Living with fun, dancing, learning, and loving.
Time is short
but eternity is forever.

Branch 32

Finding our True Selves

When we think of the word "ourselves" we often don't know what it really means.

We may think we do, but if we believe that we are just our behaviour, we don't yet understand who we deeply are.

Some people put on facades, but that's not who they are, that's just who they are pretending to be at that time.

Everyone has a beautiful, deeper side to them, but we show it in different and unique ways.

We may think that to be ourselves, we just do what we like to do, or be who we think we want to be. But the only time we can honestly be who we are, is when we are our true selves. Then we can dive deeper inside to understand more of who we are, and who we are to become.

After we have reflected on that, then we can have a better understanding of our true selves, as well as how we want to be around others.

By doing this, we will discover more of what our true self is, which we can keep discovering throughout our life.

Poem on
Finding Our True Selves

We are flowers
opening petals
revealing heart's smiles.
Connecting to others
beyond ourselves
as we unfold.

Branch 33

Self-Esteem

Self-esteem is something that everyone struggles with. Everyone is going through different things, and throughout life, we all feel changes in our minds and bodies.

When we feel low self-esteem, it may be because we don't feel as good as anyone else, or maybe we failed an assignment and our tutor is upset with us.

Sometimes we don't know what to do and might be experiencing sadness or depression, or feel ashamed to be ourselves, or we live with a sense of not feeling good enough for anyone. I have days when I feel like that, when I believe that others don't see me for who I am, and I don't think I belong.

Sometimes I say to my parents that I am not feeling good enough. It could be from the way someone is treating me, or just how I am interpreting their actions.

I think it's important not to be too hard on ourselves, otherwise we aren't living, we are merely existing.

We also need to learn not to worry too much about what others think, by remembering our accomplishments and that our blossoming is life-long.

Poem on
Self-Esteem

Living behind facades of security

unsure when to come out and explore.

But is there a right moment…

Yes

it's always now!

Branch 34

Bullying

A bully is someone who is secretly afraid of what other people might think about them, so they turn into falsely inflated personalities, who become lost in themselves.

It's very hard for a parent to see their children getting bullied. The reason the bully is behaving like that however, is because they feel threatened or jealous of another's seemingly good life or situation.

Yet bullies can often go through hard times themselves and they might not want to let others into their private world, because of a sense of shame.

When I went to school, I got bullied. I got left out a lot and excluded from most things in group activities. I just didn't fit in at school because everyone wanted to be in the cool, popular group. But I just wanted to be myself, so I wasn't interested in the cool group. I just wanted to live like a kid while I could.

I still live a little like that way now, because I like to be who I am. So when I realise I'm not being myself, I try to pull myself back into line.

Have you ever been bullied? What did you do to get through it?

I think it's really important to be your naturally, beautiful self. And then you will find that good people will come to you when they have had enough of bullies, or of people acting falsely.

Poem on
Bullying

No one likes a bully

bossing the scene.

So together we can grow

and connect

to be truly

who we want to be.

Branch 35

Controlling

When people get into arguments with family members or friends, there are reasons why they behave like that. But there is one reason that seems to come up a lot, and that's about wanting control.

People behave in this way when they have something going on underneath, which makes them want to try and control others, as well as their external circumstances. But secretly, they may actually be embarrassed about how they are acting.

I think that when we see over-the-top controlling behaviour, we can reflect on its' deeper roots, and learn to be less like that ourselves.

Sometimes we all just need to have some space, and maybe a little walk in the woods, or sit on a beach, or perhaps even lie down and reflect on how that situation first arose.

Poem on Controlling

Our controlling thoughts

cannot control the Sun

or the waves

or the wind

or other people.

But we can let go

let them be

and fly free.

Branch 36

Food

Health is one of my favourite topics. I have always been into a healthy diet and being fit, happy and feeling good in my body.

When I eat a salad or a meal including a lot of vegetables, I feel just right, not too full, not hungry enough for another snack, but just right. I love my salads, veggies and smoothies. My family call me the 'Flavour Queen' because of the different ways I mix ingredients!

I was brought up to live healthily by my beautiful parents. I have been a vegetarian all of my life. I love being vegetarian, and not being a consumer of an industry that is cruel to animals.

I know that sometimes people give me looks or put me down for being vegetarian, but I just focus on what's important to me, and not let it affect my choices in life.

My family and I aren't the type of vegetarians that push it onto others, we just think that what people choose to eat is their decision.

We all follow our own paths, and one day we may connect and realise that any previous disagreements we had were simply due to ignorance.

Poem on
Food

Plants lovingly sprout
all over the Earth.
Yummy celery and mangoes
nuts and seaweed
carrots and berries
rice and potatoes.
How can we not love
their bountiful harvest?

Branch 37
Decision Making

To make the right decision, we need a clear and relaxed mind.

We want to make the right decision based on what is best, which at times may not be what we think we initially wanted.

We also know that if we choose something because of someone else, then it may not be right for us.

I know that sometimes when I'm making decisions, I can make them based on other people's views to please them. But is that the best thing to do?

I think that peer pressure or any kind of pressure from others can get to us sometimes, and I think that's part of the reason we may have trouble standing up for ourselves.

At the end of the day, I believe that to live a happy and peaceful life, we need to be kind to ourselves. We also need to make sure we are making wise and well-thought-out decisions, not just for the short term, but also for the long term too.

The lesson needed here, is to deeply tune into what's best for you.

Poem on
Decision Making

Making decisions

and realising the compass of truth

in moments of realisation.

But let's remember

not to say goodbye to our dreams

or we may lose

our true way.

Branch 38

Taking Risks

We all need to take risks at times in life, and taking risks can be exciting! Just because it's a little out of our comfort zone and something we wouldn't normally do, doesn't mean we won't like it!

I want to take more risks in life, to see who I can become through them.

When people take risks, it may cause an adrenaline rush, which is great.

I know that when I do something out of the ordinary, I feel proud of myself. It opens my mind to other worlds I wouldn't usually think about or encounter.

But there is also a warning….sometimes us teenagers can take dangerous or careless risks. So I want to stress that you try the higher, more truthful risk of authentically being yourself, rather than following someone or something that is unhealthy, dangerously exciting, cool or fashionable.

Poem on
Taking Risks

Climbing a mountain
seeing our surroundings
within our lives
with fresh eyes.
Knowing in our hearts
that we can finally see
a way that leads
towards new visions.

Branch 39

Spirituality

Spirituality is a beautiful part of life to know and deeply understand.

When we hear the word 'Spiritual' many people think of religion and religious practices. Yet true spirituality is more down to earth, because the Earth itself can inspire us.

Spirituality peacefully connects us and allows us to recognise the beauty of life through its many different fields and colours.

Being spiritual opens us to a deeper awareness and reveals that we can reflect and see things through the many windows of reality.

If we truly focus and put our energy into the moment, we realise that we will never have this moment again, so let's not take it for granted. Instead, let's be grateful for every second we are alive.

I think this simple act of awareness will take you a long way, if you start thinking, acting and feeling like that, and alongside it, your gratitude for life will also expand.

Poem on
Spirituality

Spirituality is the essence

of why we are here.

Pausing to reflect

opens a state

of present awareness

if we stop living

such busy lives.

Branch 40

Beliefs

Me and my family live a simple and relaxed life, because this is what we choose to believe is right for us. Don't get me wrong, our lives can be busy at times, but we try to live in such a way that money doesn't dictate how we live.

I think that other people may see us as being a bit out there, since my parents homeschool me, and that we're also vegetarians, amongst many other things.

We want to live without harming animals or damaging the Earth if possible. Occasionally, other people can be judgmental about our choices, yet we don't tell them how to live. At times this can make us feel like outsiders, but we wouldn't have it any other way if it meant compromising the life we live.

I believe there is a God, but I'm not super religious, I just think that we all have a light around us, and a simple smile can open the light in our hearts. You may disagree with me on that, but that's okay, because everyone has a different view from where they stand, and how they see the world.

Yet, how great is it when you find people who believe in and value the same things as you do? And when you do, you can feel happy that you have someone to relate with and connect on a deeper level.

To me, that means so much.

Poem on

Beliefs

A purple flower blooms its purply colour
and stays true to itself.
We know that other flowers
have different colours
which makes them all unique.
Every human is just as rare
and blooms their own
individual colours.

Branch 41

Community

I love our communities here in Byron Bay, Mullumbimby and the other towns in northern New South Wales, Australia, where I live. Many of us are connected by similar interests, which unite our passions through love, kindness, truth, respect and the environment.

Of course, it's not perfect, but we attempt to live our lives in balance, with a smile.

I think that when we say the word 'Community' we feel a sense of familiarity and belonging. Community is about being together, being generous and welcoming everyone.

We had some bad floods in our region a few years ago and the local community helped each other enormously. Our family made bulk meals for those affected by the floods. and we also helped with the cleanup.

My family have always lived in beautiful communities and have made some special bonds with loving friends. I think that if you don't come from a big family, like me, you can create a new family in your community by meeting and making new friends.

Surely, it's preferable to support each other in our fast-changing world. What do you think?

Poem on
Community

We are one
under the Sun and the Moon.
Each of us can bring our love
to lift a community to light
as we open and deepen
Into larger families.

Branch 42

Wanting More

As we grow up, we often want to have everything we see. We want everything that other kids have, including the latest trends and styles. Then once that trend or style is finished, it's onto the next, and the next, and so on.

Occasionally, we might realise that we have wasted our money, or our parent's money, on foolish things, just so we can be with the in-crowd, or fit in with kids in the community or at school.

I used to be a little like that when I was younger. I remember I once saw a child who had a cool bear, and then I wanted the very same 'cool' bear. But these days, I have learned better. I like to buy and wear things that I genuinely like and want, not just because others have or wear it too. If people don't like my style, then that's not a problem. I know that when I am buying something for myself, I now tune in to what I truly want.

Sometimes I feel that I do want more, but then I wake up and realise, that the best things to have and to be grateful for, are each other, our family and friends, our home, our food, the special things we treasure, the infinite joys of nature, and life itself. What more could I possibly want?

Poem on
Wanting More

If we realised how much we consumed

from nature

we would probably be amazed

and maybe sad.

The Earth is so abundant

yet it cannot satisfy greed.

We may eventually understand

that what we deeply want

is already in front of our eyes

inside the simple pleasures

and beauty of life.

Branch 43

Positivity

To wake up feeling positive is a powerful start to the day.

If we wake up upset, then we are setting ourselves up for an unpleasant day ahead.

I know that when I wake up anxious or agitated, then I've started the day badly. But sometimes I can change that mindset and end up having a great day. It just depends on how we see life and ourselves in life's picture.

If you communicate to yourself that you want to be positive, then you can be. If you are upset, then you will definitely be upset. Everyone can change their response if they truly want to.

We are blessed to live on planet Earth, and we can be thankful for the beauty we experience about us. We can be grateful for our families and friends. We can be content with ourselves and just be happy for no reason.

Sometimes people ask me why I'm laughing, but I am just laughing because I am genuinely happy and thinking positive thoughts.

I also know that when I feel love, I feel blessed, and I realise that I'm doing the best thing for myself and others by living in a happy, positive way.

Now it's your turn!

Poem on
Positivity

Awakening from my bed

with a charge of positivity.

Arising to experience

an inner peace

wanting to reach

beyond my fingertips

and my heart.

Branch 44

What's Real or Fake

How can we tell the difference between what's real and what's fake?

For me personally, I often have an inner sense when I know I'm not being myself, or when someone else isn't being their true self.

There are many reasons why we act like that, and it's okay. Sometimes, it might just mean that we don't want people to know what's going on for us, or maybe we feel a little insecure in ourselves.

For example, when we see others appearing overly confident, they may actually be experiencing the opposite. For me, when I am insecure or shy, I know that I don't want people to truly see me. So I might, for instance, fake a smile, or hide beneath my words. I don't like it, but we all do it from time to time.

This can be a difficult topic to raise because some people don't want anyone to know who they are. It could be because they have a sad past, which they don't want others to know about. Or maybe they are just insecure and embarrassed about their lives, and the decisions they've made in life.

However it's up to you to discover who you think is being genuinely real or fake, and work out the kind of people you want in your life. Yet be aware that it is only through real people and real things that we can know the truth of the world.

Poem on
What's Real or Fake

We look through the windows

of our eyes

but what do we see?

Do we truly see ourselves?

Do we truly see others?

And do we wonder

what's real?

Branch 45

Anger

Being able to control my anger is something I sometimes struggle with. It can slowly build within me and I don't even realise how much it affects me or my family. I need to improve at controlling my anger and become more aware of it, but I think that this may be a life-long quest for me and perhaps for many of us.

Anger is something that plenty of people struggle with, and many don't fully understand why they are angry.

But I think that if we can feel how someone else is experiencing their emotions, then we can change our perspective, by simply doing things like putting ourselves in their shoes, looking through their eyes and feeling through their heart.

Sometimes we may need to have a debrief with ourselves and understand why we act in particular ways. We might not immediately know the answer, but it will eventually come to us, and occasionally at the strangest times.

We all have daily struggles in life and need to soothe our anger in ways that suit us, yet without being self-destructive or destructive to others.

Anger can build up through emotions such as frustration, impatience, fear and hurt.

But I have a technique that I know can help you if you struggle with this emotion sometimes.

If you are upset or angry, I find the best thing to do is simply exaggerate it. You'll find that you can't make it worse, so it soon leaves, and you'll be free again.

This technique lets out all of your toxic chemicals, as well as your anger. So next time it happens, try this technique and let me know if it worked for you!

Poem on
Anger

Anger rages upwards
just like volcanoes explode
over those who are guilty
and those who are innocent.
Let's open our hearts
and know who we are.
Don't let rage take over
but let the pain come
into the accepting heart
of our deeper kindness
so it can disappear
before the sun sets.

Branch 46

Harmony

When we are in harmony, we realise that we have so much to be grateful for. And if we choose to live from within our inner harmony, we can be far happier, and our problems will seem less important.

The more we live in harmony, the more we can tune into and find harmony with others and with nature.

I feel harmony when I'm at ease and happy within myself. It's almost like a feeling of deep, contented sleep, yet my eyes are open. I'm just enjoying the inner harmony I feel with myself.

You can create harmony within yourself by gently closing your eyes, and feel an inner glowing smile upon your face, then say to yourself, "I'm in Harmony." This will instantly take you into harmony deeply within, and you'll also feel harmonious with your surroundings.

Poem on
Harmony

Harmony is present
in the presence of stillness
calm and silence.
Sometimes we love
or we don't love
but underneath
there is a deeper harmony.
Can we feel harmony
wanting us to join
its chorus?

Branch 47

Quiet Moments

Beneath all of the endless action in life, to just sit still in a quiet moment is one of the best things to do in life. Yet, it requires a willingness to surrender our need to be busy, and to make a time to simply sit and be still.

No one's life is perfect, and everyone has challenges and struggles, but to become aware of them in a quiet moment, is to understand why we constantly strive.

At some point, you will want to connect with the deep peace and the quiet moments that are readily found on a beach, in a forest, in a valley or on a mountaintop.

Once you've found this stillness and quiet space, then you can truly think about what you most want out of your life.

Poem on
Quiet Moments

Sitting under a tree
just realising
that we're in a quiet moment
coming back to ourselves.
Aware of the beauty
of trees, sky, birds, and flowers
faintly smiling back
in wise wonder.

Branch 48

Laughter

I love to laugh, it's one of my favourite things.

Laughter releases endorphins and frees our thoughts into a more positive room in our mind. Laughter is the best therapy. I'm sure that everyone agrees that laughter makes us feel better and cheers us up. Even if we don't know why we are laughing, we instantly feel happy and more content.

When I am down, randomly laughing instantly puts my mind at ease and makes my body let go and relax.

Sometimes when I laugh for no reason, people ask, "Why are you laughing?" But why can't I just laugh for no reason?

If we look at the world with laughter-filled eyes, lots of things can seem funny, and the funny side of life is always a better place to be don't you think?

What makes you laugh?

Poem on
Laughter

Laughter is like a balloon
inflating our life
making our worries and pains seem small
and our lives sweeter
more simple and fun.

Branch 49

Self-Reflection

Self-reflection is something I occasionally struggle with.

Reflecting on ourselves can sometimes bring us into a state of embarrassment or regret. It can be hard to admit when we are in the wrong, so reflecting upon our behaviour can be challenging.

The easiest thing to do is just ignore or not admit things to ourselves, or others, about how we may have acted, but this doesn't help in the long run. Instead, a good thing to keep in mind is that everyone makes mistakes, and we are all human.

Sometimes it can seem like we're the only ones in the wrong, but trust me, others feel it too.

It's good to remember that we aren't alone, and that we can learn about ourselves and life in general with good friends. This in turn, will create a safe space and the opportunity for self-reflection.

Poem on
Self-Reflection

Our eyes see more
than what we see.
We can reflect upon ourselves
with inner eyes
to see inside our hearts
about what we think, say and do.

Branch 50

Truth

Truth is simply being honest with ourselves, others and with life.

If we are fully honest with ourselves, we know at times that we could have been more truthful with those around us.

Being truthful can take time, and it can sometimes be a lot to digest, because it can involve making difficult changes.

Sometimes we can cover up the fact that we know we aren't being true to ourselves; so we put up a facade, and don't see that truth can be hidden under the influences of peer pressure, popular trends, or just avoidance.

When I went to school, I found it extremely hard to be true to myself. Yet, when I tried, no one seemed to like me for just being me, so I withdrew and came across as shy to my teachers and peers.

But in truth, I'm not a shy person.

When we had the school drama plays each year, that was my time to shine, and people were amazed by my confidence. I would get lead roles, fill in for other students, and even got to choreograph some dance routines.

So regardless of what happens in our lives, or who you come across as, it's up to each of us to make sure that we stay true to ourselves, as much as we can. And hopefully, sooner or later, others will see us for who we truly are.

Poem on
Truth

Truth can come in ways we hadn't imagined.
When we lie to ourselves
we know in our hearts
that no lying words can change the facts.
Yet learning to be truthful
comes with inner knowing.

Branch 51

Maturity

When we are young, all we want to be is older, act older, feel older, and most of all, look older. But to enjoy our lives as children is just as much fun as growing up. Children can have a carefree, fun life, but when they become adults, they often want to be younger.

It's important to appreciate the special times we will never have again. Every day and every experience is a little different. We will never have the same moment or feelings ever again. So let's make sure we keep our special memories alive.

For me, growing up was a blast! I was always playing, smiling and eating, and I didn't want to lose the fun of being a kid.

Whether we are a child or an adult, it's important to let our inner child out into the open by being spontaneous, fun-loving, adventurous and sometimes, silly.

As we mature, there is a certain feeling of sadness knowing we are all going to grow old one day, and eventually die. But if we think of that all the time, we aren't being in the present, and experiencing what's happening in this moment.

Maturing can be hard, especially when we don't want to grow older, take on responsibilities and start cleaning our act up. Growing old can even seem terrible or overwhelming to young people, but if we think about it, we should feel very thankful that our bodies continue for so long. When I see older people, I want to go and introduce myself and I love seeing their big smiles when I visit them.

Over the years, I have become friends with older people that have been lovely and made me feel special. It's special because all my family live far away, and my beautiful Granny who lived close to us, unfortunately, passed away not so long ago. So to talk to older people and connect with them in the way I do, warms my heart. I truly hope you get to experience the beauty of an older friend as well.

I hope when I grow old, that a younger person will make friends with me. Older people are great listeners and they are usually interested in what we have to say. So next time you see someone older, go up and say hi, or even just smile at them, trust me it will make their (and your) day.

Poem on
Maturity

Our immature and mature selves
create different pathways.
Our young mind wants to stay young
attached to childhood ways
but like a tree
we continue to grow higher
building stronger roots
to help our maturity
reach to the sky.

Branch 52
Wonders of Life

When I think of life, I think about it with wonder.

The wonders of life appear during those special moments when we get the chance to experience things in our life that inspire us.

If we take in the world around us, we are soon captivated by how and why we came here, as well as who we came here for.

The world is an incredible place that we can sometimes take for granted, but when we experience our lives lovingly in the present, it is easier for us to understand so many more things.

Often our lives are fast-paced, and filled with so much that we rarely take in the wonders of our lives. And when we get stuck in a rut, we can become ungrateful for what we do have.

For me, if ever I feel like time is getting away from me, or I feel weak or burdened with stress, I go for an inspiring walk in nature, to find a little sheltered spot, where I close my eyes and just be in the present moment. The feeling I have afterwards is like a refreshing, energising wave passing through my body, bringing relaxation and contentment to my life.

So please remember my teen friend, that you are a wonder of life, a playful child of the Earth, and a light-filled soul from the universe.

Poem on
Wonders of Life

Life is a constant prayer
made from our everyday thoughts.
What we see and choose
guide our lives
as we experience Earth's harvest.
Yet wonder, joy and gratitude
show us
what we want to become:)

To you, wherever you are on Earth (or maybe even beyond on another planet, ha ha)... thank you for reading and being part of My Teen Friend...

love

Sunee

www.ingramcontent.com/pod-product-compliance
Lightning Source LLC
Chambersburg PA
CBHW042319090526
44583CB00025BA/3142